Joy Harjo

She Had Some Horses

Thunder's Mouth Press
New York

Published in the United States by Thunder's
Mouth Press. 632 Broadway, 7th Floor
New York, N.Y. 10012

Design by Bob Feie

Cover painting "Memories of Ruffian" by
Sherman Drexler

Acknowledgment is gratefully given to the
following publications in which some of these
poems originally appeared.

Magazines:
*Heresies, Spawning the Medicine River, Contact
II, Corn Soup, Frontiers, Conditions, The Beloit
Poetry Journal, Cedar Rock, Greenfield Review,
River Styx, Midwest Alliance Newsletter, National
Women Studies Newsletter*

Anthologies:

*Artists For Survival, Coyote's Journal, Songs
From Turtle Island, Native American Literature*
(Twayne U.S. Authors Series), *The Woman Poet*

This publication made possible by a grant
from the Illinois Arts Council.

Library of Congress Cataloging in Publication
Data:

Harjo, Joy.
She had some horses.

Poems.
I. Title.
PS3558.A62423S5 1982 811'.54 82-17064
ISBN 1-56025-119-0

Distributed by
Publishers Group West
4065 Hollis Street
Emeryville, CA 94608
(800) 788-3123

For Meridel LeSueur and for my
Great Aunt Lois Harjo Ball 1906 – 1982

And For All the Beautiful Horses

Thanks to the National Endowment
for the Arts for their support

Contents

Introduction by Greg Sarris

In my tribe, many of the medicine people, or Indian doctors as we call them, have been women. Strong women, women for whom the dark clouds of an oftentimes horrendous history of oppression and loss have neither eclipsed nor mitigated the light and strength of their vision. Their's is a vision that has sustained us always as a people. I can see them now, brave women, effortlessly gentle, effortlessly strong, their eyes clear. Essie Parrish, tall and straight, a medicine pole elaborately designed with stars and crescent moons in each hand, as she stands before the centerpole and tells the crowd gathered in the roundhouse of her Dreams, her language alive and rich. Mabel McKay, holding a cocoon rattle as she sits, bent over a patient, explaining the nature and history of the person's illness. "I have songs," Mabel told me, "songs that speak to the disease. It is living, the disease; so I have to know it, work with it, before I cast it out. I have songs for all that."

Joy Harjo is a strong woman, and she has songs. The poems in this collection chart a path of healing, woman healing, woman unafraid to stand before the ills about us in this world—poverty, the disenfranchised and dispossessed, internalized oppression—and see them, learn their ways, illuminate them so they might lose their hold over us and be cast off. What enables so many of these ills to thrive and replicate themselves in countless ways over time is fear. It is no surprise then that Joy titles the first poem in this collection "Call it Fear." Straight away she names the devil.

> There is this edge where shadows
> and bones of some of us walk
> > backwards . . .
>
> There is this edge within me
> > I saw it once

And from this poem, she moves forward, seeing more and naming what she sees.

In *Survivors,* the first of four sections into which the collection is divided, Joy sees and names not only what plagues us, as in the poem above, but also what helps us. For Joy the world is timeless, and any present situation or predicament, whether healthy or not, cannot be extricated from the past that has born it and continues to inform it. To know the present, we must know what is behind and underneath us. As she says, "And the ground spinning beneath us / goes on talking." She writes in a poem entitled "Anchorage" of an Athabascan grandmother "who is buried in an ache / in which nothing makes / sense;" buried not unlike her ancient village "underneath the [city's] concrete." In "New Orleans," Joy "look[s] for evidence / of other Creeks, for remnants of voices." With a memory that "swims deep in the blood," she sees:

> De Soto
> having a drink on Bourbon Street,
> mad and crazy
> dancing with a woman as gold
> as the river bottom.

Love and a sense of God in all things, the essence of respect for all of creation, also help in our movement toward well being and survival. Joy notes in "One Cedar Tree:"

> And I eat, breath, and pray to some strange god
> who could be a cedar tree
> outside the window.

The poems in the second section, *What I Should Have Said,* become more personal, more conversational, as Joy speaks to lovers and friends honestly, as she puts fear and inhibition aside to name and explain what she otherwise would not have said. Hence, the straightforward first lines of the title poem: "There's nothing that says you can't / call." In the third section, *She Had Some Horses,* the themes of wholeness and honesty come together; in fact, become interdependent as the poet not only identifies all aspects of herself, but also works to claim them, accept them as living parts of her one self.

> She had some horses she loved.
> She had some horses she hated.
>
> These were the same horses.

Horses in all colors and shapes, horses of love, of hate, those we escape on, those that race through your head, your heart, those you own, those who own you, Joy writes of them, calls them by name; all that she has explored earlier in the book she gathers now in the shape and form of horses, horses she—and all of us—can see as clear as the words she has used to describe them. And now that she has known and worked with these horses, now that she has identified the disease—Call It Fear—that has kept her from knowing and understanding them before, she can cast the disease out. Appropriately, the last of the four sections

contains only one poem, its title poem, "I Give You Back," for it says all
that she needs to close her song-filled ceremony. She begins:

> I release you, my beautiful and terrible
> fear. I release you.

Herein is a journey, an awakening, a woman straight and tall, clear-
eyed.
Follow her.

The Power of Horses

I do not know how to explain the horses, how to tell you about the genesis of the poems, or the poem *She Had Some Horses*. I am asked often about these poems, to elaborate on the process, the history, the mythic sense, the horses. I have changed as much as these poems have through the years. Nothing ever stays the same, whether it be poems or humans. When I look back over the many lives between then and now I remember a very young woman at her typewriter, entering the field of imagination with a great trust, even wildness. And there were the horses, shimmering in the sun and rain on the battleground of gains and losses, always revealing the possibility of love.

Each collection of poetry makes a force field of energy. When creating you give yourself over to it. In the fiercest moments of imagination the artist may not know where they are going, the how and when of it, and it doesn't matter. What matters is the process regenerates and meaning shifts at every turn. The meaning of horses shifts at every turn. When I wrote the poems that were published as a book in 1984 I needed the the power of horses. This collection was how I came to know it and them, and perhaps this was the only way the horses could appear at that time—through the poetry.

I did not grow up intimately with horses. There were laws against keeping them in the neighborhood in which we lived in Tulsa, Oklahoma. My father caused a scene when he butchered deer from bowhunting after hanging them from the one tree in our yard. Large animals were not present except as packaged meat in the grocery store.

Horses were present in images in paintings in our home and in the myths and history of the tribe and the state of Oklahoma. They also ran through my dreams as if to thread my life together when it appeared broken, unthreadable. We no longer traveled by horseback. My father's truck ran on horsepower. Horses of flesh, blood and spirit were restricted by asphalt roads and highways. We drove by them on the way to the lake, to Okmulgee or to somewhere else. We watched the horses from a distance. They stood behind fences watching the world stretching in the direction of cities, loped across patches of prairie often next to pumping oil wells, daring humans to consider a different road.

I knew the stories of horses and our family's relationship to them. Evidence of horses was an ornately-beaded saddleblanket that had belonged to my grandmother Naomi Harjo, my father's mother. I knew of her through her belongings, her paintings, which included a near life-size portrait of Osceola, another leader of the Muscogee people who never surrendered to the U. S. government. She died shortly after my father was born. I found comfort in this horse blanket, a blanket she had traded for on her travels. Its beauty was meant to decorate the back of a horse and said something about the family, the woman who beaded it. There was a horse it was intended for, a horse who had dignity and caused the blanket to be beaded for it, a horse who was loved. When I was near that blanket I knew that someone had graced this earth who had brought beauty here. I knew something of the soul of my grandmother. I missed her, as my father did. I missed the horses.

There is a history of horses from this side of my family. We are descended from Monahwee, a leader of the Muscogee people when we were still in the lands now known as Alabama and Georgia. When Tecumseh, the Shawnee leader came south to gather peoples to take part in the great alliance for justice, he conferred with Monahwee who was in agreement that our tribal nations would be stronger if joined together to stand against the travesty of destruction and loss that was assaulting the tribal nations in the east. Monahwee is best known in history books written by non-Muscogees as the leader of the Battle of Horseshoe Bend, an armed conflict against Andrew Jackson and the U.S. government against the forceful removal of our peoples from our homelands. This conflict rallied Creeks, Seminoles and associated Africans against this injustice.

In my family Monahwee is known for his magic with horses. My Aunt Lois Harjo said he was gifted in the ability to travel on a horse. He could leave for a destination at the same time as everyone else, but arrive before anyone, a feat impossible in linear time.

The world doesn't always happen in a linear manner. Nature is much more creative than that, especially when it comes to time and the manipulation of time and space. Europe has gifted us with inventions, books and the intricate mechanics of imposing structures on the earth, but there are other means to knowledge and the structuring of knowledge that have no context in the European mind.

When the explorer Magellan traveled around the world by ship, he stopped at Tierra del Fuego. The indigenous people who resided there could not see the huge flags of his ships as they docked out in the natural harbor. They had not previously imagined such structures and could not see them. Conversely, neither could European explorers see the particular meaning of indigenous realities.

History books call Monahwee a horse thief. He could capture horses easily. What they don't say is that horses knew him, relished his smell, his manner. He didn't steal them, he didn't have to—they wanted to follow him and did, from the corrals of the European immigrants, from neighboring enemy tribes.

I come from a people who are taught to forget nothing. I believe that

7

every thought, every word, every song or horse that existed makes a mural of existence that gives form to this one we find ourselves in. The construction of a word will draw forth the thing itself. The flank of a horse or the nicker will bring the horse into view. One horse will evoke the history and mythical construct of horses. The love of horses will make horses appear, as will the fear of them. The heart is the generator of all manner of ideas, including horses.

Recently a young woman of the longhouse people of the northwest coast had her coming-of-age ceremony. In preparation for this ceremony she fasted. During this time of fasting she dreamed, and was given a song in honor of this powerful place of transition. When she sang this song, the oldest women, the ones who knew her great-grandmother and the songs of her great-grandmother cried in recognition when they saw the persistence of meaning born out in this young woman. The song this young woman sang, in the shadow of the Boeing Company plant, as the salmon are being diminished, and new chemicals are being invented, was the song of this great-grandmother, a song the young woman had never heard before until it was given to her in the dream.

In that manner the horses approach the pages of this book and enter. They ride out from history, tied to the collective history of my family, the tribe, and are the ability to travel unfettered by fear, by the fury of our houses burning behind us. They become the book, grace it with the power of horses.

I traveled to the Battle of Horseshoe Bend battleground last year to pay homage to the struggle for justice that marks my family. I walked the grounds for two days, knowing that if I could make sense of the battle I could make sense of the history of America. Behind the front lines of the tribe was a village made up of remnants of towns of Muscogees who sought harbor together because they had been forcibly moved from their homes by immigrants who took their lands and houses for their own. The women and children were sequestered there as the men fought, the loop of the Tallapoosa River behind them. The village was attacked and burned from behind, by Jackson's Cherokee allies aligned with Jackson's forces, while the ground troops by superior force of weapons and numbers overran the warriors, killing women and children, too. It was in truth, a massacre. This was never told in any account of the battle I had read or heard, rather this was the "decisive battle" that won Andrew Jackson his popularity, his presidency. His image is proudly displayed at the visitor's center as is Monahwee's. Monahwee suffered seven shot wounds, but survived by sheer force of will and love, for the people.

Before the writing of the book *She Had Some Horses* I was on a road trip between Albuquerque and Las Cruces. It was quiet except for the long howls of wind running through the canyons and the hum of the efficient motor of my small truck. Then the horse appeared to me. First I smelled this horse of memory, appearing from the six generations back to Monahwee. I was aware of a million details all at once, of this horse, of our old connection, of how we had once lived and died together. We communed for several miles as tears ran down my face. It is with this appearance of my old friend that I mark the beginning of the book.

The power of horses continues to surround us. My cousin Donna Jo Harjo was a champion barrel racer, has the gift with horses that Monahwee demonstrated and though she lives on a scant retirement check has at least one horse. Once she woke herself up from a dream repeating his name when she didn't know his name or of his gift with horses. My son's name Phil is derived from an English word meaning lover of horses. He is a natural horseman. Most recently we held a ceremony for my youngest granddaughter, Desiray Kiara Chee. The horses appeared from the knowledge of the fire to surround her.

We continue despite strange turns of history, as we always have. Everyday new songs are being created, new poems and new horses. This book, then, too is meant to be part of the ongoing act of acknowledgement and regeneration.

Joy Harjo March 1997

1
Survivors

Call It Fear

There is this edge where shadows
and bones of some of us walk
                              backwards.
Talk backwards. There is this edge
call it an ocean of fear of the dark. Or
name it with other songs. Under our ribs
our hearts are bloody stars. Shine on
shine on, and horses in their galloping flight
strike the curve of ribs.
                              Heartbeat
and breathe back sharply. Breathe
                              backwards.
There is this edge within me
                    I saw it once
an August Sunday morning when the heat hadn't
left this earth. And Goodluck
sat sleeping next to me in the truck.
We had never broken through the edge of the
singing at four a.m.
                    We had only wanted to talk, to hear
any other voice to stay alive with.
                    And there was this edge—
not the drop of sandy rock cliff
bones of volcanic earth into
                    Albuquerque.
Not that,
          but a string of shadow horses kicking
and pulling me out of my belly,
          not into the Rio Grande but into the music
barely coming through
                    Sunday church singing
from the radio. Battery worn-down but the voices
talking backwards.

Anchorage
for Audre Lorde

This city is made of stone, of blood, and fish.
There are Chugatch Mountains to the east
and whale and seal to the west.
It hasn't always been this way, because glaciers
who are ice ghosts create oceans, carve earth
and shape this city here, by the sound.
They swim backwards in time.

Once a storm of boiling earth cracked open
the streets, threw open the town.
It's quiet now, but underneath the concrete
is the cooking earth,
                        and above that, air
which is another ocean, where spirits we can't see
are dancing   joking   getting full
on roasted caribou, and the praying
goes on, extends out.

Nora and I go walking down 4th Avenue
and know it is all happening.
On a park bench we see someone's Athabascan
grandmother, folded up, smelling like 200 years
of blood and piss, her eyes closed against some
unimagined darkness, where she is buried in an ache
in which nothing makes
                        sense.

We keep on breathing, walking, but softer now,
the clouds whirling in the air above us.
What can we say that would make us understand
better than we do already?
Except to speak of her home and claim her
as our own history, and know that our dreams
don't end here, two blocks away from the ocean
where our hearts still batter away at the muddy shore.

And I think of the 6th Avenue jail, of mostly Native
and Black men, where Henry told about being shot at
eight times outside a liquor store in L.A., but when
the car sped away he was surprised he was alive,

....

no bullet holes, man, and eight cartridges strewn
on the sidewalk
                    all around him.

Everyone laughed at the impossibility of it,
but also the truth. Because who would believe
the fantastic and terrible story of all of our survival
those who were never meant
                    to survive?

What Music

I would have loved you then, in
the hot, moist tropics of your young womanhood.
Then
        the stars were out and fat every night.
They remembered your name
                        and called to you
as you bent down in the doorways of the whiteman's houses.
You savored each story they told you,
and remembered
            the way the stars entered your blood
                                at birth.
Maybe it was the Christians' language
                    that captured you,
or the bones that cracked in your heart each time
you missed the aboriginal music that you were.
But then,
        you were the survivor of the births
of your two sons. The oldest one envies you, and the other
wants to marry you. Now they live in another language
in Los Angeles
            with their wives.
And you,
        the stars return every night to call you back.
They have followed your escape
            from the southern hemisphere
                            into the north.
Their voices echo out from your blood and you drink
the Christians' brandy and fall back into
        doorways in an odd moonlight.
                    You sweat in the winter in the north,
and you are afraid,
                sweetheart.

Rain

Bobby flew out from his body
   on Nine Mile Hill.
You could say it was a Navajo semi
   careening down the earth
or his wife, pregnant and drunk
   who caused his lick of death

But what captured him was a light in the river
   folding open and open
blood, heart and stones
   shimmering like the Milky Way.

And then it rained.
What went down sucked the current,
took hold.

Now southern California falls into the ocean.
Now Phoenix struggles under water.

Something has been let loose in rain;
it is teaching us to love.

For Alva Benson, And For Those
Who Have Learned To Speak

And the ground spoke when she was born.
Her mother heard it. In Navajo she answered
as she squatted down against the earth
to give birth. It was now when it happened,
now giving birth to itself again and again
between the legs of women.

Or maybe it was the Indian Hospital
in Gallup. The ground still spoke beneath
mortar and concrete. She strained against the
metal stirrups, and they tied her hands down
because she still spoke with them when they
muffled her screams. But her body went on
talking and the child was born into their
hands, and the child learned to speak
both voices.

She grew up talking in Navajo, in English
and watched the earth around her shift and change
with the people in the towns and in the cities
learning not to hear the ground as it spun around
beneath them. She learned to speak for the ground,
the voice coming through her like roots that
have long hungered for water. Her own daughter
was born, like she had been, in either place
or all places, so she could leave, leap
into the sound she had always heard,
a voice like water, like the gods weaving
against sundown in a scarlet light.

The child now hears names in her sleep.
They change into other names, and into others.
It is the ground murmuring, and Mt. St. Helens
erupts as the harmonic motion of a child turning
inside her mother's belly waiting to be born
to begin another time.

And we go on, keep giving birth and watch
ourselves die, over and over.
And the ground spinning beneath us
goes on talking.

Backwards

The moon that night was thrown
off the bridge, the one near Mesita
the tracks crawl under—
I was driving over when I saw it;
white skeleton laying on the
                        blood ground,
fallen moon rolling up
                        the bone railroad
whirring of soft seeds and thunderstorms
caught in stiff skin rattles.

Something tries to turn the earth
around. Blue dawn to the yellow west.
California to New York.
This has been going on
since I don't know when,
                        baby.

". . .when the dance is over, sweetheart
I will take you home in my one-eyed Ford. . ."

The moon came up white, and torn
at the edges. I dreamed when I was
four that I was standing on it.
A whiteman with a knife cut pieces
away
        and threw the meat
                        to the dogs.

Night Out

I have seen you in the palms of my hands
late nights in the bar
                      just before the lights
are about to be turned on. You are powerful horses
by then, not the wrinkled sacks of thin, mewing
spirit,
            that lay about the bar early in the day
                        waiting for minds and bellies.
You are the ones who slapped Anna on the back,
            told her to drink up
            that it didn't matter anyway.
You poured Jessie another Coors, and another one
                                          and another.
            Your fingers were tight around hers
        because she gave herself to you.
      Your voice screamed out from somewhere in the
darkness
            another shot, anything to celebrate this deadly
        thing called living. And Joe John called out to bring
another round, to have another smoke, to dance dance it good
because tomorrow night is another year—
                              in your voice.
        I have heard you in my ownself.
        And have seen you in my own past vision.
                    Your hearts float out in cigarette
      smoke, and your teeth are broken and scattered in my hands.
It doesn't end
For you are multiplied by drinkers, by tables, by jukeboxes
                  by bars.
You fight to get out of the sharpest valleys cut down into
the history of living bone.
                    And you fight to get in.
You are the circle of lost ones
                        our relatives.
You have paid the cover charge thousands of times over
with your lives
                  and now you are afraid

                        you can never get out.

The Woman Hanging From The Thirteenth Floor Window

She is the woman hanging from the 13th floor
window. Her hands are pressed white against the
concrete moulding of the tenement building. She
hangs from the 13th floor window in east Chicago,
with a swirl of birds over her head. They could
be a halo, or a storm of glass waiting to crush her.

She thinks she will be set free.

The woman hanging from the 13th floor window
on the east side of Chicago is not alone.
She is a woman of children, of the baby, Carlos,
and of Margaret, and of Jimmy who is the oldest.
She is her mother's daughter and her father's son.
She is several pieces between the two husbands
she has had. She is all the women of the apartment
building who stand watching her, watching themselves.

When she was young she ate wild rice on scraped down
plates in warm wood rooms. It was in the farther
north and she was the baby then. They rocked her.

She sees Lake Michigan lapping at the shores of
herself. It is a dizzy hole of water and the rich
live in tall glass houses at the edge of it. In some
places Lake Michigan speaks softly, here, it just sputters
and butts itself against the asphalt. She sees
other buildings just like hers. She sees other
women hanging from many-floored windows
counting their lives in the palms of their hands
and in the palms of their children's hands.

She is the woman hanging from the 13th floor window
on the Indian side of town. Her belly is soft from
her children's births, her worn levis swing down below
her waist, and then her feet, and then her heart.
She is dangling.

....

The woman hanging from the 13th floor hears voices.
They come to her in the night when the lights have gone
dim. Sometimes they are little cats mewing and scratching
at the door, sometimes they are her grandmother's voice,
and sometimes they are gigantic men of light whispering
to her to get up, to get up, to get up. That's when she wants
to have another child to hold onto in the night, to be able
to fall back into dreams.

And the woman hanging from the 13th floor window
hears other voices. Some of them scream out from below
for her to jump, they would push her over. Others cry softly
from the sidewalks, pull their children up like flowers and gather
them into their arms. They would help her, like themselves.

But she is the woman hanging from the 13th floor window,
and she knows she is hanging by her own fingers, her
own skin, her own thread of indecision.

She thinks of Carlos, of Margaret, of Jimmy.
She thinks of her father, and of her mother.
She thinks of all the women she has been, of all
the men. She thinks of the color of her skin, and
of Chicago streets, and of waterfalls and pines.
She thinks of moonlight nights, and of cool spring storms.
Her mind chatters like neon and northside bars.
She thinks of the 4 a.m. lonelinesses that have folded
her up like death, discordant, without logical and
beautiful conclusion. Her teeth break off at the edges.
She would speak.

The woman hangs from the 13th floor window crying for
the lost beauty of her own life. She sees the
sun falling west over the grey plane of Chicago.
She thinks she remembers listening to her own life
break loose, as she falls from the 13th floor
window on the east side of Chicago, or as she
climbs back up to claim herself again.

One Cedar Tree

The cedar tree outside the window
                    is one
                        of many.
What prayers are said to it?
What voices are raised
                    to sacred blue sky
            within its branches?
    Stars
            illuminate its form. The moon comes around
in a repetitious pattern,
                    and the sun
slopes down into a familiar sea.
(They know the tree must be the one god
        because of its life they are sure.)
What do I know?
            Only the prayers I send up on cedar smoke,
                            on sage.
        Only the children who are bone-deep echoes
                        of a similar life.
        Only the woman who sleeps generations
                            in the land.
            A continuum flows like births
because somehow
            the sun gallops in most mornings on the
eastern horizon.
        The moon floats familiar
                    but changing.
        And I eat, breathe, and pray to some strange god
            who could be a cedar tree
                    outside the window.

The Black Room

She thought she woke up.
Black willow shadows for walls
of her room. Was it sleep?
Or the star-dancer come for her dance?
There are stars who have names, who are
dreams. There are stars who have families
who are music. She thought she woke up.
Felt for skin, for alive and breathing blood
rhythm. For clothes or an earring she forgot to
take off. Could hear only the nerve
at the center of the bone—the gallop
of an elegant horse. She thought she woke
up. Black willow shadows for walls she
was younger then. Her grandmother's house
sloped up from the Illinois River in Oklahoma.
The house in summer motion of shadows breathed in cool
wind before rain rocked her. Storms were always
quick could take you in their violent hard rain
and hail. Gritty shingles of the roof. Rat
rat rat ratting and black willow branches twisting
and moaning and she lay there, the child that she was
in the dark in the motion. She thought she woke up.
Joey had her cornered. Leaned her up against the
wall of her room, in black willow shadows his breath
was shallow and muscled and she couldn't move and
she had no voice no name and she could only wait
until it was over—like violent summer storms
that she had been terrified of. She thought she
woke up. Maybe there were some rhythms that weren't
music; some signified small and horrible deaths
within her—and she rode them like horses into
star patterns of the northern hemisphere, and
into the west.

This morning she thought she woke up.
Alarm rang and fit into some motion, some voice
within her other being—a dream or
the history of one of the sky's other stars.
Still night in the house, she opens
herself for the dark. Black horses are slow
to let go. She calls them by name but she fears
they won't recognize hers, and if the dance
continues in nets of star
patterns
          would it be sleep?

White Bear

She begins to board the flight
　to Albuquerque. Late night.
But stops in the corrugated tunnel,
　a space between leaving and staying,
where the night sky catches

　　　her whole life

she has felt like a woman
　balancing on a wooden nickle heart
approaching herself from here to
　there, Tulsa or New York
with knives or corn meal.

The last flight someone talked
　about how coming from Seattle
the pilot flew a circle
　over Mt. St. Helens; she sat
quiet. (But had seen the eruption
　as the earth beginning
to come apart, as in birth
　out of violence.)

She watches the yellow lights
　of towns below the airplane flicker,
fade and fall backwards. Somewhere,
　she dreamed, there is the white bear
moving down from the north, motioning her paws
　like a long arctic night, that kind
of circle and the whole world balanced in
　between carved of ebony and ice

　　　oh so hard

the clear black nights
　like her daughter's eyes, and the white
bear moon, cupped like an ivory rocking
cradle, tipping back it could go
either way
　　　all darkness
　　　　　　is open to all light.

Leaving

Four o'clock this morning there was a call.
You talked Indian, so it was probably her mother.
It was. Something not too drastic, tone of voice,
no deaths or car wrecks. But something. I was
out of the sheets, unwrapped from the blankets,
fighting to stay in sleep. Slipped in and out of your
voice your voice on the line.
You came back to me. Lit cigarette blurred in the dark.
All lights off but that. Laid
down next to me, empty, these final hours
before my leaving.

Your sister was running away from her boyfriend and
was stranded in Calgary, Alberta. Needed money
and comfort for the long return back home.

I dreamed of a Canadian plain, and warm arms around me,
the soft skin of the body's landscape. And I dreamed
of bear, and a thousand mile escape homeward.

Cuchillo

cuchillo
    sky
        is blood filling up my belly

cuchillo
    moon
        is a white horse thundering down
        over the edge
        of a raw red cliff

cuchillo
    heart
        is the one who leaves me
        at midnight
        for another lover

cuchillo
    dog
        is the noise of chains and collar
        straining at the neck to bite
        the smell of my ankles

cuchillo
    silver
        is the shell of black sky
        spinning around inside
        my darker eyes

cuchillo
    dreams
        are the living bones that want out
        of this voice dangling
        that calls itself
                knife
                (cuchillo).

Skeleton Of Winter

These winter days
I've remained silent
as a whiteman's watch
keeping time
        an old bone
empty as a fish skeleton
at low tide.
It is almost too dark
        for vision
these ebony mornings
but there is still memory,
the other-sight
and still I see.

Rabbits get torn under
cars that travel at night
but come out the other
side, not bruised
breathing soft
like no fear.

And sound is light, is
movement. The sun revolves
and sings.

There are still ancient
symbols
        alive
I did dance with the prehistoric horse
years and births later
near a cave wall
late winter.

A tooth-hard rocking
in my belly comes back,
something echoes
all forgotten dreams,
        in winter.

I am memory alive
                    not just a name
but an intricate part
of this web of motion,
meaning: earth, sky, stars circling
my heart

            centrifugal.

Connection

A hawk touches down
       the humming earth before Miami,
                        Oklahoma.
     You old Shawnee, I think
             of your rugged ways
      the slick-floored bars and whiskey
      sour nights when the softer heart
                    comes apart.
The Spokane you roam isn't City of the Angels
   but another kind of wilderness.
      You speed in a Ford truck and it's five
      in the morning, the sun and dogs
                only ones up
and you go home to red earth
            when you see a hawk
    crossing wires

         touching down.

Kansas City

Early morning over silver tracks
a cool light, Noni Daylight's
a dishrag wrung out over bones
watching trains come and go.
They are lights, motion
of time that she could have
caught
          and moved on
but she chose to stay
in Kansas City, raise the children
she had by different men,
all colors. Because she knew
that each star rang with separate
colored hue, as bands of horses
and wild
          like the spirit in her
that flew, at each train whistle.
Small moments were cycles
at each sound.
                    Other children elsewhere
being born, half-breed, blue eyes,
would grow up with the sound
of trains etched on the surface
of their bones, the tracks
cutting across Kansas City into hearts
that would break into pieces
in Cheyenne, San Francisco
always on the way back home.
Early morning,
                    if she had it to do over
she would still choose:
the light one who taught her
sound, but could not hear his
own voice, the blind one
who saw her bones wrapped
in buckskin and silver,
the one whose eyes tipped up
like swallows wings
                    (whose ancestors laid this track,
                    with hers),

all of them,
their stories in the flatland belly
giving birth to children
and to other stories
and to Noni Daylight
standing near the tracks
waving
at the last train to leave
Kansas City.

The Friday Before The Long Weekend

You come in here
drunk child
pour your beer
down the drain,
"apple juice",
bullshit.
I can see you,
I can see
you, what you
are doing to yourself
is something
I can't sing about.
I can point
to the piss yellow
drops in the sink.
I can see the stagger
in your eyes
glasses askew
your voice loud
cawing
uncertain bravado
and you come in here
to be taught
to take writing
but hell,
what can I teach you
what can I do?
Something shaky and terrible
starts in my belly.
The sour reality rolls over
in my throat.
I can't do anything
but talk to the wind,
to the moon
but cry out goddamn goddamn
to stones
and to other deathless voices
that I hope will carry
us all through.

Song For Thantog
for Keith Wilson

Thantog
         you are jaguar priest
spirit of fire, of the edge of light that occurs
in the swift falling down of day
                            into night. Forever
is yours but this night I watch out the dark with you,
tend the fire with my fingers,
                       stir the cool wind
and you pray:
                   for the return of the sun

                   for the spirit of the moon

                   for life,
and, it is all good, you say
as you stand up on your hind legs, Thantog
                         and pray
that those yellow eyes in motion in the night

that those spirits behind the eyes who know us better

than our mothers
                you pray

that they come out from their hiding and devour us,

because they are fire, Thantog
they are own skin and blood
and what better life is this
than to so stand up singing
                   with no blade edge
against ourselves
other than voices
out of the fire.

Heartbeat

Noni Daylight is afraid.
She was curled inside her mother's belly
for too long. The pervasive rhythm
of her mother's heartbeat is a ghostly track
that follows her.
                        Goes with her to her apartment, to her sons'
room, to the bars, everywhere; there is no escape.
She covers her ears but the sound drums
within her. It pounds her elastic body.
Friday night Noni cut acid into tiny squares
and let them melt on her tongue.
                        She wanted something
to keep her awake so the heartbeat
wouldn't lull her back.
                        She wanted a way to see the stars
complete patterns in her hands, a way to hear
her heart, her own heart.
These nights she wants out.
And when Noni is at the edge of skin she slips
out the back door. She goes for the hunt, tracks the
heart sound on the streets
                        of Albuquerque.
She steers her car with the hands her mother gave her.
The four doors she leaves unlocked and the radio
sings softly
                        plays softly and Noni takes the hand of the moon
that she knows is in control overhead.
Noni Daylight is afraid.
She waits through traffic lights at intersections
that at four a.m. are desolate oceans of concrete.
She toys with the trigger; the heartbeat
is a constant noise. She talks softly
                              softly
to the voice on the radio. All night she drives.
And she waits
                  for the moment she has hungered for,
for the hand that will open the door.
It is not the moon, or the pistol in her lap
but a fierce anger
                  that will free her.

37

Nandia

Over McCartys
a crow flies north
near the house
you lived in with Tony.
I think of you,
see old bones of lava beds,
a train going towards
Gallup,
radio fading out
only wind, and
this dry mouth
whisper thin,
like leaves.

We traveled this road
before. Sixty-six
or other names in the time
you breathed. Knew
red rock mesas, Indian tea
stalks dried and empty
and the hardened
black ashes
of the Malpais.

You took me once
to an older part of earth
I'd never seen—
where monsters were born
and killed.
They sacrificed everything
and nothing
for a taste of this
life.

I remember
you held your baby
tight.
He was yours and Tony's—
a point inbetween
hot baked earth
and Oklahoma.

We crawled a fence
found a barren
Laguna corral where years
back sheep birthed and slept
and were kept by an old man
and woman whose children
have grown old in L.A.

To the Rio Puerco
deep blood of silence
where the sun fell   .
to the western horizon
and your voice and mine
echoed laughter;
carried children.

Now footprints are mere ghosts
washed over in the river
and there are wings
slapping wind
that force sound through me.

I drive this road again
my children older
and this ache
        this trembling ache
haunts me endlessly
like you.

Remember

Remember the sky that you were born under,
know each of the star's stories.
Remember the moon, know who she is.
Remember the sun's birth at dawn, that is the
strongest point of time. Remember sundown
and the giving away to night.
Remember your birth, how your mother struggled
to give you form and breath. You are evidence of
her life, and her mother's, and hers.
Remember your father. He is your life, also.
Remember the earth whose skin you are:
red earth, black earth, yellow earth, white earth
brown earth, we are earth.
Remember the plants, trees, animal life who all have their
tribes, their families, their histories, too. Talk to them,
listen to them. They are alive poems.
Remember the wind. Remember her voice. She knows the
origin of this universe.
Remember you are all people and all people
are you.
Remember you are this universe and this
universe is you.
Remember all is in motion, is growing, is you.
Remember language comes from this.
Remember the dance language is, that life is.
Remember.

Vision

The rainbow touched down
"somewhere in the Rio Grande,"
we said. And saw the light of it
from your mother's house in Isleta.
How it curved down between earth
and the deepest sky to give us horses
of color
          horses that were within us all of this time
but we didn't see them because
we wait for the easiest vision
                    to save us.

In Isleta the rainbow was a crack
in the universe. We saw the barest
of all life that is possible.
Bright horses rolled over
and over the dusking sky.
I heard the thunder of their beating
hearts. Their lungs hit air
and sang. All the colors of horses
formed the rainbow,
                    and formed us
watching them.

New Orleans

This is the south. I look for evidence
of other Creeks, for remnants of voices,
or for tobacco brown bones to come wandering
down Conti Street, Royale, or Decatur.
Near the French Market I see a blue horse
caught frozen in stone in the middle of
a square. Brought in by the Spanish on
an endless ocean voyage he became mad
and crazy. They caught him in blue
rock, said
           don't talk.

I know it wasn't just a horse
                   that went crazy.

Nearby is a shop with ivory and knives.
There are red rocks. The man behind the
counter has no idea that he is inside
magic stones. He should find out before
they destroy him. These things
have memory,
           you know.

I have a memory.
                   It swims deep in blood,
a delta in the skin. It swims out of Oklahoma,
deep the Mississippi River. It carries my
feet to these places: the French Quarter,
stale rooms, the sun behind thick and moist
clouds, and I hear boats hauling themselves up
and down the river.

My spirit comes here to drink.
My spirit comes here to drink.
Blood is the undercurrent.

There are voices buried in the Mississippi
mud. There are ancestors and future children
buried beneath the currents stirred up by
pleasure boats going up and down.
There are stories here made of memory.

I remember DeSoto. He is buried somewhere in
this river, his bones sunk like the golden
treasure he traveled half the earth to find,
came looking for gold cities, for shining streets
of beaten gold to dance on with silk ladies.

He should have stayed home.

>   (Creeks knew of him for miles
>   before he came into town.
>   Dreamed of silver blades
>   and crosses.)
And knew he was one of the ones who yearned
for something his heart wasn't big enough
to handle.
>   (And DeSoto thought it was gold.)

The Creeks lived in earth towns,
>   not gold,
>   spun children, not gold.
That's not what DeSoto thought he wanted to see.
The Creeks knew it, and drowned him in
>   the Mississippi River
>   so he wouldn't have to drown himself.

Maybe his body is what I am looking for
as evidence. To know in another way
that my memory is alive.
But he must have got away, somehow,
because I have seen New Orleans,
the lace and silk buildings,
trolley cars on beaten silver paths,
graves that rise up out of soft earth in the rain,
shops that sell black mammy dolls
holding white babies.

And I know I have seen DeSoto,
                having a drink on Bourbon Street,
                mad and crazy
                dancing with a woman as gold
                as the river bottom.

Nautilaus

This is how I cut myself open
—with a half pint of whiskey, then
  there's enough dream to fall through

      to pure bone and shell
      where ocean has carved out

warm sea animals,
            and has driven the night
            dark and in me

            like a labyrinth of knives.

She Remembers The Future

"We are closer than
blood", Noni Daylight
tells her. "It isn't
Oklahoma or the tribal
blood but something more
that we speak."

(The otherself knows
and whispers
to herself.)

The air could choke, could
kill, the way it tempts
Noni to violence, this
morning. But she needs
the feel of danger,
                    for life.

She feels the sky
tethered to the changing
earth, and her skin
responds, like a woman
to her lover.
It could be days, it could
be years, White Sands
                    or Tuscon.

She asks,
          "Should I dream you afraid
          so that you are forced to save
          yourself?

          Or should you ride colored horses
          into the cutting edge of the sky
          to know

          that we're alive
          we are alive."

2
What I Should Have Said

Untitled

Either a snail's moist web
of moonlight, or someone's
hot breath at four a.m.
when the night has been
too much, has eaten
you whole.
This is my life.
It has been
sifted through the bones
of my body, through
blood.
It is all that
I have.

What I Should Have Said

There's nothing that says you can't
call. I spend the weekdays teaching
and moving my children from breakfast
to bedtime. What else, I feel like a traitor
telling someone else things I can't tell
to you. What is it that keeps us together?
Fingertip to fingertip, from Santa Fe
to Albuquerque?
I feel bloated with what I should say
and what I don't. We drift and drift, with
few storms of heat inbetween the motions.
I love you. The words confuse me.
Maybe they have become a cushion
keeping us in azure sky and in flight
not there, not here.
We are horses knocked out with tranquilizers
sucked into a deep deep sleeping for the comfort
and anesthesia death. We are caught between
clouds and wet earth
and there is no motion
                              either way
no life
to speak of.

Moonlight

I know when the sun is in China
because the night shining other-light
crawls into my bed. She is moon.
Her eyes slit and yellow she is the last
one out of a dingy bar in Albuquerque—
Fourth Street, or from similar avenues
in Hong Kong. Where someone else has also
awakened, the night thrown back and asked,
"Where is the moon, my lover"?
And from here I always answer in my dreaming,
"the last time I saw her was in the arms
of another sky".

Jemez

Sometimes it is like
facing the dreamer
who knows the you
of blood and stars—
and you talk out
the winter,
horses neighing
at the razor sky.

And the dreamer leaves.

Maybe you never see
the dreamer again—
but coming toward you
are Jemez Mountains
opened red
        like the sun going down
against
    soft earth.

Late Summer Leaving

I woke up and turned on the light.
You were dreaming
                        of white birds.
                                    Hibernating.
        Your face tilted a soft angle
                        to the light.
                                    Even in
your sleep you sense direction.
            Your eyes are closed to the brightness
                        but you breathe in sun
            like sunflowers do.
(The sense of light is like another
            kind of touch,
                            like air and water to the skin.)
I am dressed now and see myself walk
        away from you
                        in an arc.
                                I see a war shield on the wall
        round and feathers leaning out.
There are geese in the north
                        cleaning their wings
        in preparation for flight south,
                            and I can hear you
another voice in your dreaming
                        like birds
talking about some return home.
You turn your head
                        one more time before I go.
        Your body shifts itself like a boat
                        on a strange tropical sea.
You face east.
                    The sun
            comes up over the Sandias on star time.
It is another year,
            another morning.
I watch it return in you
            and say one last song to return home on.

Motion

We get frantic
in our loving.
The distance between
Santa Fe and Albuquerque
shifts and changes.
It is moments;
it is years.
I am next to you
in skin and blood
and then I am not.
I tremble and grasp
at the edges of
myself; I let go
into you.
A crow flies over
towards St. Michaels,
opens itself out
into wind.
And I write it to you
at this moment
never being able to get
the essence
       the true breath
in words, because we exist
not in words, but in the motion
set off by them, by
the simple flight of crow
and by us
       in our loving.

Alive

The hum of the car
is deadening.
It could sing me
to sleep.

I like to be sung to:
deep-throated music
of the south, horse songs,
of the bare feet sound
of my son walking in his sleep.

Or wheels turning,
spinning
spinning.

Sometimes I am afraid
of the sound
of soundlessness.
Like driving away from you
as you watched me wordlessly
from your sunglasses.
Your face opened up then,
a dark fevered bird.
And dived into me.
No sound of water
but the deep, vibrating
echo
        of motion.

I try to touch myself.
There is a field
of talking blood
that I have not been able
to reach,
not even with knives,
not yet.

"I tried every escape",
she told me. "Beer and wine
never worked. Then I
decided to look around, see
what was there. And I saw myself
naked. And alive. Would you
believe that?
Alive."

Alive. This music rocks
me. I drive the interstate,
watch faces come and go on either
side. I am free to be sung to;
I am free to sing. This woman
can cross any line.

Your Phone Call At 8 AM

Your phone call at eight a.m. could
have been a deadly rope.
All the colors of your voice
were sifted out. The barest part flew
through the wires. Then tight-roped
into the comfort of my own home,
where I surrounded myself with smoke
of piñon, with cedar and sage.
Protected the most dangerous places,
for more than survival, I always
meant. But what you wanted, this morning
you said, was a few words
and not my heart. What you wanted. . .
But the skeleton of your voice
clicked barely perceptible,
didn't you hear it?
And what you said you wanted
was easy enough, a few books
some pages, anything, to cancel
what your heart ever saw in me that you didn't.
But you forgot to say that part.
Didn't even recognize it when it
came winging out of you—
the skeleton's meat and blood,
all that you didn't want to remember
when you called at eight a.m. . . . .
But that's alright because
this poem isn't for you
but for me
                after all.

The Poem I Just Wrote

The poem I just wrote is not real.
And neither is the black horse
who is grazing on my belly.
And neither are the ghosts
of old lovers who smile at me
from the jukebox.

The Returning

I don't know
who Hugo Wolf is.
I don't even know who
you are, maybe coyote who
has fooled himself
again, and me
into believing
the trickery of the heart.
What I am saying is
that it smells like almost
rain, and I am here in this office
set off from Cerrillos Road. I
study and read poems and try to put
myself in them.
But you keep coming back
scratch your fingers at the
door and that voice that you always
had, arching into me.
Raw red cliffs that you
stumbled down into your own shadow
haven't kept you away, or soft
red lights and strange electrical
music that I play. I am always
in danger. A painting of Blues Man
hangs on the wall in front of me.
The sky swirls down against
a nippled earth in a drawing
that Leo sent, Che, and these words
that I keep trying to follow back
to their original patterns.
But your half-grin
is the only image that comes clear.
All the words lead to that, even
the coming rainsmell sets your voice
not mine, into motion. You can
call yourself anything you want. Maybe
you *are* Hugo Wolf going mad the way Bukowski
said it. Or maybe you are my own life
scheming desperately to climb
back in.

September Moon

Last night you called and told me
about the moon over San Francisco Bay.
Here in Albuquerque it is mirrored
in a cool, dark, Sandia sky.
The reflection is within all of us.
Orange, and almost the harvest
moon. Wind and the chill of the colder
months coming on. The children and I
watched it, crossed San Pedro and Central
coming up from the state fair.
Wind blowing my hair was caught
in my face. I was fearful of traffic,
trying to keep my steps and the moon was east,
ballooning out of the mountain ridge, out of smokey clouds
out of any skin that was covering her. Naked.
Such beauty.
        Look.
We are alive. The woman of the moon looking
at us, and we looking at her, acknowledging
each other.

3
She Had
Some
Horses

She had some horses.

She had horses who were bodies of sand.
She had horses who were maps drawn of blood.
She had horses who were skins of ocean water.
She had horses who were the blue air of sky.
She had horses who were fur and teeth.
She had horses who were clay and would break.
She had horses who were splintered red cliff.

She had some horses.

She had horses with eyes of trains.
She had horses with full, brown thighs.
She had horses who laughed too much.
She had horses who threw rocks at glass houses.
She had horses who licked razor blades.

She had some horses.

She had horses who danced in their mothers' arms.
She had horses who thought they were the sun and their
bodies shone and burned like stars.
She had horses who waltzed nightly on the moon.
She had horses who were much too shy, and kept quiet
in stalls of their own making.

She had some horses.

She had horses who liked Creek Stomp Dance songs.
She had horses who cried in their beer.
She had horses who spit at male queens who made
them afraid of themselves.
She had horses who said they weren't afraid.
She had horses who lied.
She had horses who told the truth, who were stripped
bare of their tongues.

....

She had some horses.

She had horses who called themselves, "horse".
She had horses who called themselves, "spirit", and kept
their voices secret and to themselves.
She had horses who had no names.
She had horses who had books of names.

She had some horses.

She had horses who whispered in the dark, who were afraid to speak.
She had horses who screamed out of fear of the silence, who
carried knives to protect themselves from ghosts.
She had horses who waited for destruction.
She had horses who waited for resurrection.

She had some horses.

She had horses who got down on their knees for any saviour.
She had horses who thought their high price had saved them.
She had horses who tried to save her, who climbed in her
bed at night and prayed as they raped her.

She had some horses.

She had some horses she loved.
She had some horses she hated.

These were the same horses.

II   *Two Horses*

I thought the sun breaking through Sangre de Cristo
Mountains was enough, and that
wild musky scents on my body after
long nights of dreaming could
unfold me to myself.
I thought my dance alone through worlds of
odd and eccentric planets that no one else knew
would sustain me. I mean
I did learn to move
after all
and how to recognize voices other than the most familiar.
But you must have grown out of
a thousand years dreaming
just like I could never imagine you.
You must have
broke open from another sky
to here, because
now I see you as a part of the millions of
other universes that I thought could never occur
in this breathing.
And I know you as myself, traveling.
In your eyes alone are many colonies of stars
and other circling planet motion.
And then your fingers, the sweet smell
of hair, and
your soft, tight belly.
My heart is taken by you
and these mornings since I am a horse running towards
a cracked sky where there are countless dawns
breaking simultaneously.
There are two moons on the horizon
and for you
I have broken loose.

III . *Drowning Horses*

She says she is going to kill
herself. I am a thousand miles away.
Listening.
          To her voice in an ocean
of telephone sound. Grey sky
and nearly sundown; I don't ask her how.
I am already familiar with the weapons:
a restaurant that wouldn't serve her,
the thinnest laughter, another drink.
And even if I weren't closer
to the cliff edge of the talking
wire, I would still be another mirror,
another running horse.

Her escape is my own.
I tell her, yes. Yes. We ride
out for breath over the distance.
Night air approaches, the galloping
other-life.

No sound.
No sound.

IV   Ice Horses

These are the ones who escape
after the last hurt is turned inward;
they are the most dangerous ones.
These are the hottest ones,
but so cold that your tongue sticks
to them and is torn apart because it is
frozen to the motion of hooves.
These are the ones who cut your thighs,
whose blood you must have seen on the gloves
of the doctor's rubber hands. They are
the horses who moaned like oceans, and
one of them a young woman screamed aloud;
she was the only one.
These are the ones who have found you.
These are the ones who pranced on your belly.
They chased deer out of your womb.
These are the ice horses, horses
who entered through your head,
and then your heart,
your beaten heart.

These are the ones who loved you.
They are the horses who have held you
so close that you have become
a part of them,
                an ice horse
galloping
        into fire.

V Explosion

The highway near Okemah, Oklahoma exploded.

There are reasons for everything.

Maybe   there is a new people, coming forth
               being born from the center of the earth,
               like us, but another tribe.

Maybe   they will be another color that no one
               has ever seen before. Then they might be hated,
               and live in Muskogee on the side of the tracks
               that Indians live on. (And they will be the
               ones to save us.)

Maybe   there are lizards coming out of rivers of lava
               from the core of this planet,

                              coming to bring rain

               to dance for the corn,
               to set fields of tongues slapping at the dark
               earth, a kind of a dance.

But maybe the explosion was horses,
                         bursting out of the crazy earth
near Okemah. They were a violent birth,
flew from the ground into trees
                         to wait for evening night
mares to come after them:

....

then	into the dank wet fields of Oklahoma
then	their birth cords tied into the molten heart
then	they travel north and south, east and west
then	into wet white sheets at midnight when everyone sleeps and the baby dreams of swimming in the bottom of the muggy river.
then	into frogs who have come out of the earth to see for rain
then	a Creek woman who dances shaking the seeds in her bones
then	South Dakota, Mexico, Japan, and Manila
then	into Miami to sweep away the knived faces of hatred

Some will not see them.

But some will see the horses with their hearts of sleeping volcanoes
and will be rocked awake
                    past their bodies

                    to see who they have become.

4

I Give
You
Back

I Give You Back

I release you, my beautiful and terrible
fear. I release you. You were my beloved
and hated twin, but now, I don't know you
as myself. I release you with all the
pain I would know at the death of
my children.

You are not my blood anymore.

I give you back to the soldiers
who burned down my home, beheaded my children,
raped and sodomized my brothers and sisters.
I give you back to those who stole the
food from our plates when we were starving.

I release you, fear, because you hold
these scenes in front of me and I was born
with eyes that can never close.

I release you
I release you
I release you
I release you

I am not afraid to be angry.
I am not afraid to rejoice.
I am not afraid to be black.
I am not afraid to be white.
I am not afraid to be hungry.
I am not afraid to be full.
I am not afraid to be hated.
I am not afraid to be loved.

to be loved, to be loved, fear.

Oh, you have choked me, but I gave you the leash.
You have gutted me but I gave you the knife.
You have devoured me, but I laid myself across the fire.

I take myself back, fear.
You are not my shadow any longer.
I won't hold you in my hands.
You can't live in my eyes, my ears, my voice
my belly, or in my heart my heart
my heart   my heart

But come here, fear
I am alive and you are so afraid
                    of dying.

Joy Harjo was born in Tulsa, Oklahoma in 1951, and is of the Creek Tribe. She left Oklahoma to attend high school at the Institute of American Indian Arts, and later received her B.A. from the University of New Mexico, and her M.F.A. from the Iowa Writers Workshop. She has taught Native American Literature and Creative Writing at the Institute of American Indian Arts and Arizona State University, and has participated in numerous workshops across the United States. She serves on the Board of Directors for the National Association of Third World Writers and is on the Policy Panel of the National Endowment for the Arts. She is the author of *The Last Song*, and *What Moon Drove Me To This*, both collections of poetry. Currently she lives in Santa Fe and is working on a screenplay and a new poetry collection.